Masterpieces: Artists and Their Works

Picasso

by Shelley Swanson Sateren

Consultant:
Joan Lingen, Ph.D.
Professor of Art History
Clarke College
Dubuque, Iowa

Bridgestone Books
an imprint of Capstone Press
Mankato, Minnesota

Bridgestone Books are published by Capstone Press
151 Good Counsel Drive, P.O. Box 669, Mankato, Minnesota 56002
http://www.capstone-press.com

Library of Congress Cataloging-in-Publication Data
Sateren, Shelley Swanson.
  Picasso / by Shelley Swanson Sateren.
  p. cm.—(Masterpieces: artists and their works)
  Includes bibliographical references and index.
  Summary: Discusses the life, works, and lasting influence of Pablo Picasso.
  ISBN 0-7368-1122-2
  1. Picasso, Pablo, 1881–1973—Juvenile literature. 2. Artists—France—Biography—
Juvenile literature. [1. Picasso, Pablo, 1881–1973. 2. Artists. 3. Painting, French. 4. Painting,
Modern—20th century—France. 5. Art appreciation.] I. Picasso, Pablo, 1881–1973. II. Title.
III. Series.
ND553.P5 S3826 2002
709'.2—dc21   2001003736

Editorial Credits:
Blake Hoena, editor; Karen Risch, product planning editor; Heather Kindseth, cover
  designer and interior designer; Katy Kudela, photo researcher

Photo Credits:
Art Resource, cover (left); Art Resource/Giraudon, 18
Fogg Art Museum, Harvard University Art Museums, USA/Bequest from the Collection of
  Maurice Wertheim, Class 1906/Bridgeman Art Library, 8
Hulton/Archive/Getty Images, cover (right)
Mary and Leigh B. Block Charitable Foundation; restricted gift of Maymar Corporation and
  Mrs. Maurice L Rothschild; through prior gift of Mr. and Mrs. Edwin E. Hokin; Hertle
  fund, 1954.270. The Art Institute of Chicago, 20
Musee Picasso, Paris, France/Bridgeman Art Library, 14
Museo Nacional Centro de Arte Reina Sofia, Madrid, Spain/Bridgeman Art Library, 16
Museo Picasso, Barcelona, Spain/Bridgeman Art Library, 6
Private Collection/Roger-Viollet, Paris/Bridgeman Art Library, 4
Pushkin Museum, Moscow, Russia/Bridgeman Art Library, 10
The Museum of Modern Art, New York. Acquired through the Lillie P. Bliss Bequest, 12

1 2 3 4 5 6 07 06 05 04 03 02

Table of Contents

Pablo worked on art almost every day of his life. He began drawing at age 2 and painted until his death in 1973.

Pablo Picasso

Pablo Picasso (1881–1973) is one of the most important artists of the 1900s. He helped develop several new styles of art.

In the early 1900s, Pablo began an art movement called Cubism. Cubists flattened and simplified the shapes of the objects they painted. They often painted objects in sections. The different sections showed all sides of the objects.

Pablo helped invent new art methods such as collage and assemblage. He created a collage by attaching objects like newspaper and chicken wire to paintings. Assemblage is a type of sculpture using everyday objects. Pablo once used a bicycle seat and handlebars to make a bull's head and horns.

Pablo's experiments with art styles led to abstract art. People and objects often do not look lifelike in abstract art. Instead, artists give an impression of people and objects in their creations.

Pablo painted *First Communion* when he was 14 years old. The
man on the left side of the painting resembles Pablo's father, José.

Young Pablo

Pablo Ruiz y Picasso was born in Malaga, Spain, on October 25, 1881. His father was José Ruiz Blasco. His mother was María Picasso y Lopez.

José was an art teacher and a painter. He encouraged Pablo to draw and paint. He also signed up Pablo for art classes. At age 14, Pablo finished a painting of a pigeon that his father had started. After seeing the painting, José thought that Pablo was more talented than he was. José then decided to give up painting and concentrate on Pablo's art education.

José wanted Pablo to have a classical art education. Classical art is created in the style of ancient Greek and Roman art. Classical paintings show people and objects exactly the way they look.

But Pablo wanted to work with different styles of art. In 1900, he decided to visit Paris, France, with his friend Carlos Casagemas. In Paris, artists were experimenting with new art styles.

This version of *Mother and Child* was painted during Pablo's Blue
Period. The mother's hands and feet appear to be unnaturally long.

Blue Period

Casagemas died soon after the visit to Paris. Pablo lived in Barcelona, Spain, following his friend's death. This time was hard for Pablo. He was saddened by Casagemas's death. People also bought few of his paintings. Pablo often did not have money for food or art supplies. He even had to burn some of his drawings to keep warm.

This time of Pablo's life became known as his Blue Period (1901–1903). During his Blue Period, Pablo used a great deal of blue in his paintings. Blue is considered the color of sadness.

The color blue seemed to fit the people Pablo painted. He painted people suffering from loneliness and hunger. He often painted beggars and poor people.

Pablo began to develop his own style during his Blue Period. He did not make people look real in his paintings. He painted them with extra long fingers, arms, and legs. He made their bodies thin and bony. Their faces often looked like masks.

Picasso

Pablo painted this version of *The Family of Saltimbanques* (comedians) in 1905. The figure on the left side of the painting may be a self-portrait of Pablo.

Rose Period

In 1904, Pablo decided to move to Paris. He met many artists and writers there. He often went to cafes and parties to talk about art and writing with them.

During this time, Pablo met and fell in love with Fernande Olivier. Pablo's mood improved shortly after he met her. He no longer felt as sad. Pablo's paintings also changed. He began to paint with reds, pinks, and oranges instead of blues. This change marked the beginning of his Rose Period (1904–1905).

The subjects Pablo painted also changed. Many of his paintings during this time showed jesters, circus acrobats, and clowns.

Art collectors were more interested in Pablo's Rose Period paintings than his Blue Period paintings. They liked the happier subjects and colors of his Rose Period. Pablo began to sell more paintings. Soon, he was earning enough money to live comfortably.

Pablo was studying African masks when he painted *Les Demoiselles d'Avignon*. The two women on the right have faces that look like African masks.

Cubism

In 1907, Pablo painted *Les Demoiselles d'Avignon*. Many people did not understand this painting. They thought it was strange. Pablo had painted the women's bodies in flat shapes.

George Braque was one of the few people who praised Pablo's painting. At the time, Braque and Pablo were experimenting with similar ways of painting. Soon, they were painting together and sharing ideas.

Braque and Pablo began the Cubist art movement. Cubists broke down people, objects, and landscapes into simple shapes in their art. The shapes often looked like building blocks. The artists put these shapes together in different ways as they painted. The shapes showed the front, back, and sides of objects or people at one time.

Pablo often painted two eyes on one side of a person's face. He moved the mouth and nose around on the face. This placement showed the front and sides of a person's face at the same time.

Pablo used a rope to frame *Still Life with Caned Chair*. The bottom left section of this collage is a piece of cloth that looks like part of a chair.

Collage

In 1917, Pablo met Russian ballerina Olga Koklova while working on the ballet *Parade*. *Parade* was about circus people. Pablo had agreed to make the sets and costumes for the ballet.

In 1918, Olga and Pablo married. They had a son named Paulo in 1921.

In the 1920s, most art critics and dealers had accepted Cubism. People bought many of Pablo's paintings. He was becoming one of the most successful artists of the time.

Pablo continued to experiment with art styles. One day, he would paint a Cubist painting. The next day, he might create a classical style of painting.

Some of Pablo's experimentation led to collage. Collage comes from the French word "coller," which means "to paste." Pablo glued newspaper, rope, or cloth to his paintings. The images he painted in his collages were not lifelike. But he tried to make them look real by pasting real objects to the paintings.

Guernica is 11.5 feet by 25.6 feet (3.5 meters by 7.8 meters). The painting shows a dying horse and a woman in a burning building. On the left side of the painting, a mother screams as she holds her dead child.

Guernica

Pablo and Olga had a troubled marriage. They often argued and Pablo eventually left her.

In 1927, Pablo met Marie-Thérèse Walter. In 1935, she and Pablo had a daughter named Maya.

In 1936, civil war broke out in Spain. Several Spanish military leaders attacked the Spanish government. German leaders helped the Spanish military leaders. In 1937, German pilots bombed Guernica, Spain. About 2,000 people died during this attack.

Pablo supported the Spanish government. He sent money to Spain to help people suffering because of the war. Pablo was angry about the bombing of Guernica. The bombing inspired him to paint *Guernica*.

In *Guernica*, Pablo showed the horrors of war. He used only black, white, and gray paint. He used these colors to represent death and destruction. In 1937, *Guernica* was displayed at the World's Fair in Paris. It is one of Pablo's most famous paintings.

Pablo used a ball to make the ape's body for the statue *The Ape and Her Young.* He used coffee cup handles for the ape's ears.

Assemblage

In 1943, Pablo met Françoise Gilot. She and Pablo had two children together. Claude was born in 1947 and Paloma was born in 1949. But Françoise left Pablo in 1953.

In 1954, Pablo met Jacqueline Roque. In 1961, they married. Pablo spent the rest of his life with her.

During the mid-1900s, Picasso created a new type of sculpture called assemblage. Sculptors usually carved statues from rock or formed them from clay. But Picasso used everyday objects to create his sculptures. He used forks, bicycle seats, pieces of wood, or other objects that he found. Assemblage also is known as found-object art.

His son's toy car inspired Pablo to make the sculpture *The Ape and Her Young.* The car became the ape's head. Marbles in the car's front windows were the eyes. Pablo created the idea that everyday objects could be turned into art.

In 1921, Pablo painted this version of *Mother and Child*. He created this painting in a classical art style. He also made the figures appear as if they were made out of stone.

Picasso's Fame

Because of his fame, Pablo often was asked to paint special works. In the 1950s, officials from the United Nations asked him to paint a wall in its new building in Paris. The United Nations is an organization that promotes world peace. The wall was 33 feet (10 meters) square. Pablo made the painting on 40 separate panels. Pablo then had the panels placed on the wall.

In 1967, Pablo's painting *Mother and Child* sold for $500,000. No other living artist had ever received this much money for one work of art.

Pablo died at his home in Mougins, France, on April 8, 1973. He was 90 years old. Pablo worked on a painting the night before he died.

Today, many museums own Pablo's paintings and sculptures. Both Paris and Barcelona have museums dedicated to Pablo. The Museum of Modern Art in New York also owns many of Pablo's works.

Important Dates

1881—Pablo is born in Spain on October 25.

1901—Pablo's Blue Period begins.

1904—Pablo's Rose Period begins.

1907—Pablo paints *Les Demoiselles d'Avignon*; this painting is considered the first Cubist painting.

1914—World War I begins.

1918—Pablo marries Olga Koklova.

1921—Pablo's son Paulo is born.

1935—Pablo's daughter Maya is born.

1937—Town of Guernica is bombed; Pablo paints *Guernica*.

1939—World War II begins.

1947—Pablo's son Claude is born.

1949—Pablo's daughter Paloma is born.

1961—Pablo marries Jacqueline Roque.

1973—Pablo dies on April 8.

Words to Know

assemblage (uh-SEM-blahzh)—an art form using everyday objects to make sculptures
classical (KLASS-uh-kuhl)—in the style of ancient Greek or Roman art
collage (kuh-LAHZH)—an artwork made by gluing materials such as paper, cloth, and yarn to a surface
critic (KRIT-ik)—someone who reviews art, books, or movies
Cubism (KYOOB-iz-uhm)—an art style in which artists break objects, people, and landscapes into simple shapes
sculpture (SKULP-chur)—something carved or shaped out of stone, wood, metal, marble, or clay

Read More

Lowery, Linda. *Pablo Picasso.* On My Own Books. Minneapolis: Carolrhoda Books, 1999.
Pfleger, Susanne. *A Day with Picasso.* Adventures in Art. New York: Prestel, 1999.
Wallis, Jeremy. *Pablo Picasso.* Creative Lives. Chicago, Ill.: Heinemann Library, 2001.

Useful Addresses

Montreal Museum of Fine Arts
P.O. Box 3000, Station H
Montreal, QC H3G 2T9
Canada

Museum of Modern Art
11 West 53rd Street
New York, NY 10019

Internet Sites

The Artchive—Pablo Picasso
http://www.artchive.com/artchive/ftptoc/picasso_ext.html
On-line Picasso Project
http://www.tamu.edu/mocl/picasso
Picasso: The Early Years, 1892–1906
http://www.boston.com/mfa/picasso

Index